TRY NOT TO LAUGH CHALLENGE

Joke Book

13 YEAR OLD Edition

Howling Moon Books

Try Not to Laugh Challenge ™

13 Year Old Edition!

Rules:

Pick your team, or go one on one.

Each team should face each other & make eye contact.

Take turns reading jokes to each other.

You can make silly faces, funny sound effects, goofy voices, wacky movements or anything laughable!

When your opponent laughs or cracks a smile, you get a point!

First team to win 3 points, or the most points, **Wins!**

Note:
You can make the game short with a total of 3 points, or longer with a total of 10 points, or more. You can split the book up and play in rounds, or go through the whole book until you reach the end if you want...it is up to you!

How much sleep does a 13 year-old need?

Just five more minutes!

Why do 13 year-olds cross the road?

Because they saw other teens doing it on social media!

Why was the laptop annoyed?

Because people kept pushing its buttons!

What do you call a pirate who skips school?

Captain Hooky!

Why shouldn't you tell jokes about dead cellphones?

They just don't WORK!

What do cow farts smell like?

Dairy Air!

Why did the selfie go to prison?

It was framed!

When can a colander hold water?

When you put ice in it.

Why do teenagers travel in groups of three?

Because they can't even!

Why don't 13 year-olds worry about answering chain emails?

Because 13 is already unlucky!

What do you always get on your birthday?

A year older!

What happens if you drop your cellphone in your bubble bath?

It starts syncing!

What do you call a pimple on your knee?

AK-nee!

What allows you to go from one story to another?

A staircase!

Why did the teen go back to bed?

Because she was told to follow her dreams!

Why did the droid win the dance contest?

Because he was a dancing machine!

How do dogs keep the peace?

With PAW and Order!

Why was the teen given detention?

Because he SWORE he did his homework!

What kind of pillow should you sleep on before a test?

A MEMORY foam pillow!

How do you know if the APPS on your iPhone are panicking?

They all SHAKE right before you delete them!

Why are bees dangerous?

Because they have at least four black belts!

What is a swimmer's favorite exercise?

POOL-ups!

Why shouldn't you spell the word "part" backwards?

It is a TRAP!

Why was the pen so dim-witted?

Because it wasn't a Sharpie!

What happens when you squirt ketchup in your eye?

In HEINZ sight, you should have pointed the bottle the other way!

Where does "The Cloud" go on vacation?

An Airbnb!

Why doesn't the unicorn eat large meals?

She is more of a GRAZER!

Why didn't the chef slice his cheese?

He had GRATER plans for it!

Why couldn't the book stand up for itself?

It didn't have a SPINE!

What do you give a 13 year-old for their birthday?

A four-leaf clover!

What helps Santa's elves get around when they get older?

Candy CANES!

Why aren't cats creative?

Because their owners tell them
NOT to THINK about going OUTSIDE
the litter BOX!

What did the kids think about the
teacher who was mean to everyone?

At least he was FAIR!

Why was the calf mad at his little
sister?

Because she was being
a CATTLE-tail!

What holds a teen's wardrobe?

The floor!

Who is to blame for all the clothes on the floor?

Gravity!

Say my name and I go away.
What am I?

Silence!

What do high schoolers say to middle schoolers?

Nothing, they just text!

How do you know if you are watching too many Star War movies?

You do the Jedi hand wave at automatic doors!

Who made the number 13 lucky?

Taylor Swift!

What is a vampire's favorite sport?

CASKETball!

How do monsters predict what will
happen in the future?

They read their HORRORscopes!

Why did the pirate walk the plank?

Because he didn't have a dog!

Why can't a T. Rex take selfies?

His arms are too short!

Why can't the T. Rex clap?

They are extinct!

Why shouldn't you trust a clock?

Because TIME will tell!

How do you make a pirate mad?

Take away the p!

What's the best thing you can say
about an Avengers movie?

It is MARVELous!

What is a 13 year-old's favorite
movie?

Any movie rated PG-13!

Why did the vampire get braces?

To improve his bite!

What kind of food do you serve
at a sleepover party?

PIZZZZA!

How do hornets say hi to each other?

WASP UP?

There are some pros and cons about New Year's Eve. What is the biggest con?

CON-fetti!

What kind of food is always fooling a-ROUND?

A doughnut!

Why did the teen bring a chair home from school?

Because the teacher told him to please TAKE a seat!

Why didn't the teen get extra credit for reading the book?

It was Facebook!

How do you make a potato puff?

Chase it around the house!

What does a 13 year-old eat for breakfast?

UnLUCKY CHARMS!

When do you need a ladder?

When you go to High School!

What has 2 legs but cannot walk?

A pair of JEGGINGS!

What do you call a fake pizza?

A pepperPHONY pizza!

Why can't 13 year-olds go to some pirate movies?

Because they were rated Arrrrrr!

How do you get a teenager to talk to you?

Change the Netflix password!

What has 4 legs, but doesn't walk,
but can climb?

A ladder!

What does a cactus wear to an
important meeting?

A CAC-TIE!

What is a baseball player's least
favorite Star Wars movie?

The UMPIRE strikes back!

What is a computer's favorite
Christmas song?

TECH the Halls!

Why did the girl take a break from
texting?

Because she was saying LOL instead
of laughing!

What did the gymnast say after she tumbled down the hill?

"That's how I roll!"

Why did the cat smell so good?

She was wearing PURRfume!

Why was the bride unlucky?

Because she didn't marry the Best Man!

How do singers communicate?

With musical notes!

What do you call a 13 year-old who drinks too much water?

THIRST-teen!

Why do people like their GPS app?

Because they would be lost without it!

Why didn't the girl buy camouflage pants at the mall?

Because she couldn't find any!

Did you hear about the nun who wouldn't iron her clothes?

It was a bad HABIT!

Why can't you play Hide and Go Seek with a Pokemon?

Because one of them will Pikachu!
(peek at you)

Why did the fish say Moo?

It was farm-raised!

Why doesn't soap get in trouble?

It always makes a clean get-away!

What kind of liquid is on the track team?

Running water!

Why are geologists like a good detective?

Because they leave no STONE left unturned!

What do llamas call the end of the world?

Llamagedan!

How do teenagers help with chores?

When they let Mom know when there is no more food in the house!

What kind of clothes do lawyers wear?

Lawsuits!

Where do you go to buy a lightsaber?

The Darth Maul!

Why do annoying sailors go overboard?

Because they take it ONE STEP too far!

What car can you drive into deep water?

A Scubaru!

Why doesn't a candy store ever get in trouble?

It is full of GOODIES!

What did the teens say when they finished binge-watching a mummy series?

That's a wrap!

Why is taffy like a Wookiee?

It is CHEWY!

Why didn't the girl cry when the soda bottle fell on her foot!

Because it was a SOFT drink!

Why did the iPhone go to the dentist?

It was having a problem with its Bluetooth!

Why didn't the dog like the Roomba vacuum cleaner?

Because it keeps beating him to the food on the floor!

Why can't cats work on the computer?

They are too busy chasing the mouse around!

Why did the girl throw her monthly planner in the air?

She wanted to see her plans take off!

What kind of money do astronauts use in space?

Starbucks!

What is the name of the ghost that lives in your iPhone?

SIRI!

What did the zombie mom yell at her teen son?

"Turn down the music, you are going to wake the DEAD!"

Why don't you see giraffes in middle school?

Because they are all in high school!

What do you call a lazy hornet?

A wannaBEE!

What is Spiderman's secret identity in Iceland?

Peter Parka!

What Star Wars character drinks
the most coffee?

Java the Hut!

What do you call an iPhone that
doesn't fool around?

Dead SIRI-ous!

What do you call a broken digital
clock?

A waste of time!

Where can you ride a horse next to a bear, a lion and a tiger?

A carousel!

What is the cheapest musical instrument?

An air guitar!

It has been noticed that kids dab here and there.

Looks like they like to DABBLE in body gestures!

What is the most annoying computer message?

Your username or password is incorrect!

What is the most annoying computer question?

Are you a human?

How did the pair of dice meet?

By chance!

Why can't you trust atoms?

Because they make up everything!

What should you learn about protons?

Because they are so positive!

Why don't dogs bark at their feet?

It's not polite to talk back to your PAW!

Why should you never fart in church?

Because you will have to sit in your pew!

Why didn't the chicken cross the street?

Because there was a Chick-fil-la on the other side!

What is the fastest mammal on earth?

A TEENAGER who sees Mom or Dad pull into the driveway and the CHORES haven't been done yet!

What kind of animal lives under your bed?

A dust bunny!

What do you call a witch who keeps messing up her magic?

Miss Spell!

What kind of tree can you plant on your face?

A facePALM!

What is right in front of you but you can't see it?

Your future!

What are the coolest things to read?

FAN fictions!

What month has 28 days?

All of them!

Why is a clock mean?

Because it will not give you the time of day!

What does a girl do with a cheesy credit card?

Go on a shopping BRIE!

How do you find Will Smith in the snow?

Look for Fresh Prints!

Why did the girl buy shoes that had an alarm clock feature?

She didn't want her feet to fall asleep!

What has no beginning, no end
and no middle?

A doughnut!

Where is Frankenstein from?

All over!

I sing but I have no mouth.
I didn't move much in the past, but
now I follow you everywhere.
What am I?

A cell phone!

What do you call blue coffee?

Depresso!

On what floor does a unicorn live
in a high-rise building?

On the 13th floor!
(Both do not exist)

What do you give a computer geek
for Christmas?

A GIF basket!

Where does a bad light beam
end up?

Prism!

How do avocados communicate?

With GUAKIE talkies!

What looks like you but is not you?

A selfie.

What happens if you get shampoo in your mouth while you are singing in the shower?

It becomes a SOAP opera!

Where do people shop if they need braces?

At the GAP!

What bus cannot bring you to school?

A syllabus!

What do pilots pack for lunch?

PLANE yogurt!

What is the richest kind of dessert?

FORTUNE cookies!

Why can't you trust your jeans?

They will always pocket your money!

Why doesn't a smart car fart very often?

Because it doesn't have a lot of GAS!

What does a cheerleader eat for breakfast?

CHEER-ios!

What do you call a lightbulb reunion?

A flash mob!

What is a major milestone for babies today?

The first time they text, "Data!"

What happens when winter arrives?

Autumn leaves!

What does a cat wear to bed?

PURR-jamas!

I am planted, then dried. You
must put me in water to be enjoyed.
The longer I am wet, the stronger
I get. What am I?

Coffee!

What came out one hole and drifts into two holes?

A fart!

What liquid has emotion?

Ink!

What flips you around without moving you?

A mirror!

What do you call a cat lover?

A cat PURRson!

Why didn't the ghoul want to go out with the zombie?

Because he was a dead-beat!

Why was the cell phone wearing glasses?

It lost its CONTACTS!

What do you call a zombie doorbell?

A dead ringer!

What kind of superhero makes bread?

Spi-DOUGH man!

How do you make cool music?

Put your iPhone in the fridge!

What kind of angel has wings but can't fly?

A snow angel!

What kind of pet does a supermodel own?

A Glamour-Puss!

Where do spices go when they are feeling sick?

Dr. Pepper!

When does a car shop for an extra tire?

In his SPARE time!

What kind of dog does not bite?

A hot dog!

What kind of bee will never sting you?

A frisbee!

What do you call a broken can opener?

A CAN'T opener!

What does a lightbulb weigh?

A WATT!

What makes songs but never sings?

Musical notes!

What did the dentist say to the computer?

This won't hurt one BYTE!

What kind of boat will you never see in a lake?

A DRY one.

What do you call a cow without a map?

UTTERLY lost!

What kind of storms are female?

HER-icanes!

What do you call an old snowman?

A creek!

What is 67 + 78 + 39 + 165 + 33?

A headache!

Why do teens run around the bed?

So they can catch up on sleep!

Why did R2D2 need glasses?

So he could C3PO!

The more I show myself, the less you see. What am I?

Darkness!

What does the geometry student make on a snow day?

Snow ANGLES!

What can you serve that you cannot eat?

A volleyball!

Who is the oldest apple?

Granny Smith!

Why couldn't the teen hand in his computer science homework?

It was hacked!

Why did the teen fail his take-home open-book exam?

Google was down!

What table can you eat with?

A tablespoon!

What is the difference between today's teens and their parents?

One takes selfies and the other points the camera at others and says "Cheese!"

What do you call a teen droid in gym class?

C3BO!

Why didn't Frosty go to the Christmas party?

Because he just wanted to CHILL!

What happened when the teens hiked down the mountain?

It started out great, but it was all downhill from there!

Silly, Willy, Shrilly, or Filly. Which word does not belong?

Or!

Why were sales for exit signs down?

Because they are on their way OUT!

Why shouldn't you drink too many
unicorn frappuccinos?

It can cause a LATTE problems!

What has a head and a tail but
no body?

A coin!

What do you find at the end of
a line?

The letter e!

What do you call a jacket that is
on fire?

A blazer!

Why did the cow get a second job?

To make lots of MOOOLA!

Who can create drama out of pretty much anything?

A LLAMA QUEEN!

When are your eyes not your eyes?

When a cold wind makes them WATER!

I help you express your emotions
without using words. I am actually
quite funny.
What am I?

A poop emoji!

Available from Howling Moon Books

Available from Howling Moon Books

Available from Howling Moon Books

Available from Howling Moon Books

13 Year Old Edition

Hope you had a blast with this
Try Not to Laugh Challenge
13 Year Old Edition!

Your smile muscles can now
relax after playing with these
Corny One-Liners & Tricky Riddles!

Please consider leaving us a review
on Amazon.com. We value your
feedback & greatly appreciate
your time!

Howling Moon Books

Made in the USA
Middletown, DE
08 December 2019